Cherry Smyth is an Irish writer, living in London. Her debut
collection, *When the Lights Go Up* was published by Lagan
Press, 2001. Her anthology of women prisoners' writing, *A
Strong Voice in a Small Space* (Cherry Picking Press, 2002), won
the Raymond Williams Community Publishing Award in 2003.
She has also been published in recent anthologies of new Irish
poetry, *Breaking the Skin* (Black Mountain Press, 2002), and
Magnetic North (Verbal Arts Centre, 2006). A pamphlet, *The
Future of Something Delicate*, was published by
Smith/Doorstop, 2005.

By the same author

Poetry
When the Lights Go Up

Pamphlet
The Future of Something Delicate

As editor
A Strong Voice in a Small Space:
Writings From Women on the Inside
(Winner of the Raymond Williams Community Publishing Prize, 2003)

ONE WANTED THING

ONE WANTED THING

CHERRY SMYTH

for Abbey

Cherry Smyth

27·11·07

LAGAN PRESS
BELFAST
2006

Acknowledgements
My thanks to Peter Sansom, Janet Fisher, John Siddique, Adrian Fox, Elaine Gaston, Michael Langan, Shaun Levin, Paul Duffy, Nina Rapi, Andy Cohen, Ron and Ailna Smyth, Mark Wood, Peppe Orru, Luciano Martins and Inge Blackman. Very special thanks to Michal Sapir who deepens my way of seeing and saying.
Much gratitude to Hawthornden Castle, Fundacion Valparaiso, the Heinrich Boll Cottage and the Tyrone Guthrie Centre where some of these poems were written; and to Hugh and Noreen Clarke, Bubbles and John Gillespie, Jane Pillinger and Marie Mulholland, Marianne Klopp and Laura Hatton for generously offering their homes as mini residencies.

Thanks to the editors of the following magazines where many of these poems first appeared: Poetry Ireland Review, Magma, Staple, The Shop and The North.
And to the editors of the following anthologies: Breaking the Skin, (Black Mountain, 2002) and Magnetic North (Verbal Arts Centre, 2006).
'One Wanted Thing' was nominated for the Forward Best Poem of the Year, 2004.

Published by
Lagan Press
1A Bryson Street
Belfast BT5 4ES
e-mail: lagan-press@e-books.org.uk
web: lagan-press.org.uk

ISBN: 1 904652 37 9

Author: Smyth, Cherry
Title: One Wanted Thing
2006

Design: December

Printed by J.H. Haynes & Co. Ltd., Sparkford

for Michal

Contents

Water

is where I'm happiest,
naked, if possible, out of my depth,
my breasts going their own way,
cracks rinsed and explored,
like it's a given, a marriage
where no asking is necessary.

I dive under, hair growing ecstatic,
frondish, slower to turn back than
my head, limbs unhumiliated, strong,
feet playful. More efficient than walking,
I front crawl, breath timed, pronounced,
not slipping by unnoticed.
This is alive!

Then comes floating,
skin a guest of air.
I hold my palms just beneath
the surface, plying the tension
as if they could lift the water up
and it would not break, like love should be,
elastic, fluent, so familiar,
you can't tell if you're in it or out of it.

Lacan's Idea of Love

The fields below are frosted and the trees throw
long shadows till all I see are beautiful dark pencils.
December has scalded the mountains, stiffened
the cow parsley. Geese tow white stitches
against the trees, the treeline a snug eyebrow.
All flap, all stillness, a crow becomes a black branch.
The sun barely goes over the rise before it makes honey.

Molten sky, golden grass, my sharp northern splendour.
The magnification of a low beam reaches like a heart
into your city room, with its screen glow, its monadic quiet,
wanting you here to travel with me, show you this weather,
the cool shading that draws you. I would bestow
what I don't have: a journey, a view, an even keel,
the belonging a bird has with a tree.

Lacan said love is giving something that one doesn't have.

Painted Horses

A small coronary of fear
shot through me
when you said you wanted
someone else.
I felt deciduous, losing foliage
in a forest of evergreens,
younger, more beautiful than I,
with straight, supple spines.
For minutes, all we'd ever known
was apparitional, my ground
a moving icesheet
the bulk of it, unseen.
I wanted to splurge
on Machu Picchu, Tokyo,
saturate myself with sights
you'd never see, we'd
never talk about,
and a great wall built up
around my heart,
where you walked
to get a better view.
But that wasn't as bad
as when you said you'd
go out and find sex
if I didn't give you more,
as if I was a ticket machine
and you'd paid your entry,
or a funfair where all
the painted horses
spun round just for you.

Lone Wolf Language

In the land where she doesn't speak the tongue,
hers is quiet, lying less used,
except to eat, sing and lick her lips.
She likes living in silence in a thick coat,
where 'please', 'water' and 'thank you'
stand up like red roadside poles through deep snow.
The habits of the people are strange,
separate, but they understand a nod,
a pointing, a smile and money.
To look, learn, love and make a living—
she doesn't want much from the world,
just experience and time to write of it,
visit the shift between I and you and we,
words held with her teeth till the thaw.

In Residence

They come in clutches with remnants of paper,
creased and tucked. Rubbish to anyone else
but alive and beating as a chick to them.
Some I must gentle into my palm,
others hunt me down for a trophy.

The rhythm is early childhood,
the tick tock of the first clock,
the singsong of a group verse,
words long forgotten
but the strokes reliable as chocolate.

There's not much I can give except to say well done,
make a strong voice in a small space.

Sometimes their glee is four years old,
wild, susceptible and bright. It carries them like swifts
bearing gifts that will attend to the source.
Nested words, a small crown, soft lined,
something to hold their head up for.

On bad days, their eyes are nerveless, screened.
They don't preen. Only strip light can enter.
They've taken poison and I watch
as they tear their words into
small white pieces for the birds.

Seeing Ghosts
11th February, 2004, 11.20pm, Almeida Passage, London N1

I don't rush the dark passageway
to Milner Square, though I am pushed
to run from the bloke behind—
he is young and tall and black.
I'm ashamed that I glance back
to check his pace, to glimpse
the contours of his face,
half-hidden by his white hoodie.

Already I'm describing his eyes
—wide-set, shy, hearing clarity in my voice
as the police scribe, 'And he was very beautiful.'
I sing a made-up song that goes
Gucci...Gu- Gu- Gu- Gucci,
believing it must be wrong to attack
mid-song, a song about fashion
in a tune trying to be less white.

I cross into my dim avenue,
he dawdles at the corner of the square
as if bare fear divides us
into stories we have no use for,
like that summer in Portrush
when I outgrew the ghost train ride,
saw mechanics tame the rising corpse,
heard the human in the ghoul's howl.

Shepherd's Warning

I'm waiting for the dawn when things will look up.
I'm waiting for my sixteenth birthday to make a difference.
Found a half-smoked fag today.
Don't even smoke but it's a way
to ask for something people can give.
A light. A bit of warm.
Hunger scares them.
A girl gave me the rest of her Chinese.
I used her fork. Germs don't matter after a while.

Something old has got in my eyes.
I breathe out her name. Fionnuala.
It protects me. Fionnuala. A light.
Mammy read what I wrote.
Fionnuala's fingertips slowly stirring
the bumps down my spine like sugar lumps in hot tea.

I wrote 'lift off' in my diary.
Fionnuala put me to sleep
where I dreamed I was OK.
The wolf is back, eating my mind. It feeds on sin.
Dad off his rocker. No daughter of mine.
I shouldn't have liked it, then I wouldn't have wrote it.

One man was kind. A pound in my lap.
Cappuccino is only coffee with foam.
I thought it was more.
All the walls are down.
It's me in the world.
The nights are too long,
the length of Ireland, on foot,
with no money and old trainers.

You smell great, Fionnuala said.
We babysat, warm on the settee.
Heaven was that.
I was evil and happy. I didn't hurt anybody.
BIG FAT LEZZIE in big black letters all over my books.
I'm thin. Skinny as a rake.
How come they knew before I did?
Brown paper wrapper. Gold stars stuck on.
Heaven fallen in.

I'm more thin, hips pointy. Something got old in my eyes.
The cat dragged me in, through a hedge backwards.
I'm a sight. I smell powerful.
Hope I don't see someone I know.
I scratched at her window. Fionnuala!
They called the police.

I wish I'd followed the girls holding hands.
They do that here, sometimes. I seen it. Not just on TV.
Next ones I'll follow.
The light's changing.
The sky is pink mohair and red cushion.
I'll be sixteen tomorrow.

Shine On Sarah Lucas

Your tight little legs hang
like a fag from a dry mouth,
no toes, no head—who hurt you, Bunny?

Mucous-yellow melons
with their mapped skin,
poke from worn-sofa dreams.

Your love is a burnt tower of muscle.
Someone left your chicken hole
on the supermarket shelf.

There is no music
just the cold green pulse
of a fluorescent cock

and torrid tales of bonking
without fizz or pop.
You sit on the loo,

dressed like a bloke,
strong as beer,
smoking.

Silver Gelatin on Aluminium
for Dirk Braeckman

I got lost in a Dubrovnik hotel, came upon
a curtained doorway. I just stood and looked.
It was that way with her. I knew I was to enter
another time, like when I mislaid my diary
for days, couldn't frame my near future.

My feet were bare, the soles sooty.
I walked across her white carpet,
up her long back, leaving prints:
a dark figure at the Antrim shoreline
walking like a man. Her yellow rusty pick-up
pulling away from San Francisco airport.
Me, by the river Ouse, with swans and white legs,
too much bra showing for her. The sharp lens
of her eyes, wet from the shower, in another
borrowed bathroom. My hand in her stash
as she posed above me on the bed. Fresh
flowers beheaded on the parquet floor.

For years, we ran together, chemicals
in love with the glare of a flash on a flawed face.
Now I stand in evening rooms of soft charcoal,
sipping wine, aware of midnight, listening
for a laugh that cracks the ground.

A Hundred Thousand Welcomes

Fields swam green through the rain. Brits on the runway
crouched like rabbits. The whiff of pigs.

Driving from the airport through a checkpoint,
fearful you'd forget your name, the way you prayed.

A red light swinging ahead in total blackness.
You knew it wasn't someone in need. You slowed

not knowing who would be at the end of the gun,
a land rover, a dark diagonal across the road.

A tension you didn't know was tension ate at your neck.
You thought it was the bite of home.

You wanted to be homeless, a thousand miles away,
not creeping along a narrow road you love

with the eye of a rifle in your eye, a hedge
warping into human shape at the edge of light.

These are the things that gnawed, drove us to a city
where nights are lit, spiced and very bricked.

In Greenhill Park, hot slack still sweats and smokes.
Arms open in immense welcome on a bright porch.

Human Image

I am looking at a painting by Louis le Brocquy
of a finger-hole poked in wet cement.
Slowly, a wounded, receding face appears,
a grey mirage of head, holding the spirit captive.
The hole fastens into a mouth,
taut as a navel, screaming.

We waited for the images on television
to resolve into fiction. Watched blazing
pieces shower down the column of eyes,
kept watching until belief occurred,
somewhere behind the retina where
incomprehension burnt a dark hole.

How to carry the bulk and heft of it— this new way
to think about dying. We would anticipate
smithereens in the North, take the risk of living,
not without regard, but unguarded, attentive,
summoning forgiveness from a gap of light,
a place that could not be set in stone.

Invitation to Nuha Al-Radi

Blossoms scatter among the birdsong, the same
as a century ago, when Lady Ottoline tended
this garden, conscientious objectors turned the soil.
The parrot tulips have flopped, baring tiny dark heads.

Oranges, small as ping-pong balls,
dropped from your trees, you said.
Barium in the Baghdad air, uranium
in the water. Then eighteen-year-olds
dropped too and did not get up.

How can I enjoy the lilac's praise
for English springtime,
when young men from this shire
have murdered those you knew?

You couldn't sleep when the shelling stopped,
kept painting the portrait of your uncle,
welcomed everyone to bring their lamb,
their chicken from lost, defrosted freezers.
Who tends your orange trees, your palm trees now?

Painters have stared into the heart of this garden,
understood its refuge, its regimented beds.
Gertler and Carrington talked in greens for the poplar,
browns for the shadows making love in the pond.

You must have seen this week's pictures
of soldiers laughing over a mound of naked
bodies, must have stored them with
your gone friends, deformed babies,
the broken bridges and ruins of Suleikh.

Musicians are playing a Vivaldi concerto
in the barn. You would enjoy Garsington
if I could give it to you. You would show me
the omen in the flowering japonica if there was one.

Nuha Al-Radi is the author of Baghdad Diaries (Saqi Press)

Night Crossing

There isn't anything left in me, in the night street,
blurred through Kimmo and Tooniz, scratched

into the top window. The schoolboy next to me
twiddles his drawstring, eyes soft tarmac.

We both know the route, the stunted tags, too well.

I start reading a poem called 'Thaw', look up,
catch a sign for 'Snow Hill', a single gift.

The glass collects our breath,
squeezed in and out at each stop.

The deck rocks.
The boy swipes an arc through the fog.

An indicator blurts ahead. I zoom in
from the rain to the white reflection

of my open book, and discover I am the one
reading poetry on the evening bus,

that square of light, a bright anomaly,
weirdness I hold on to.

As this thing that separates, brings me closer
to the lost boy, the graffiti, the judder of passengers

climbing off and on, the dark orange city
beyond the rivered windows, shoring me up.

Dunfanaghy, October 2002
after the dissolution of the Northern Ireland Assembly

Sand scuffs and scatters across the estuary,
all water this morning, colourless
and shapeless as rain. A blue
too pale to survive breaks the cloud
like a face at an unlit window.

Incoming tide picks up the bruised sky
for the milky violet within a mussel shell.
The sea is all the patterns and colours
of everything it makes live. It slips
its fan, ridged as cockles over the land,
splits it into flank and shore.
The sand permits.
A changing light bleaches the oval atoll,
the deep wade darkens maroon
and the contrast splashes in my blood.

How much watching must I do
before the lesson leaves me satisfied?
Till the island is swallowed and will appear
tomorrow as a new idea in the same mind?

Then swans, a dozen or so,
tear up the grey strait of water
in an avalanche of spray
and a laugh overtakes my mouth.
Take shelter from the mind,
rest from beating against it,
the form of the body cut out by its force.

Minutes later, the birds shudder air,
stagger up thick steps of wind,

then seem to catch a current
and stream with easy elegance
out over the trees to vanish as white sky,
as if an old idea gained velocity,
lifted itself out of the picture,
a magic trick that shows how it's done
as it's done.

One Wanted Thing

You come down the steep slope
in a yellow fleece, scattering yellow
like pollen, leaning back as if
you're floating on white water,
your arms doing a wide paddle.

You are a parachute of mimosa,
in lolling command of the skis and the poles,
all joy, all ease. One wanted thing your dad left,
making you test the tiny slope at six,
take fall after fall until you got it—
the glide and balance of having control
and giving it up.

I watch from the bottom in earth shoes,
the way you open up to the drop
and rock with the mountain, just as you do
with those you love, billowing,
arms a go-go, face hot and happy,
making the snow, water, the ground, air.
You teach me how to lose the floor.

Nursing Poetry
for Adrian Fox

All I could think of for days
was the fat slug of toothpaste
the nurse fretted round your teeth
when you lost your swallow
couldn't tell liquid from air.

Under the foam, your tongue
a white seal, lay asleep
your lips
couldn't pucker or pop
couldn't spit out a pellet of blood.

You crawled your left hand heavy
as a bear's claw to the alphabet
on your lap, spelt out 'I'm alright' and
'Read "A Disused Woodshed ... "
so I can be present.'

Pause

It is the perfect winter to make ready for love,
after the salt falls for the snow,
the sky, a brief and forgiving blue,
before night hides our wrinkled afternoon.

Turn your memory slow as a bulb,
picking out dry pieces of hurt,
hold them up to the morning light,
the emptiness, breathing out.

Strengthen your wrists to bear the weight
of your torso as it becomes adored,
believe in the quiet a song needs
to make everything listening stand on end.

Presence of Mind
after Carol Rhodes' painting 'Carpark, Canal', 1994

There are no people in the watery green,
a mass of slate angled under a dirty sky.
There's poetry in it because it was chosen.
Flatness can give beauty room.

Objects come after receiving colours
like a scent before you name it.
A carpark, a golfcourse with flags
and dunes in the distance, a path,

a wall, some shrubby trees. Steps
cut into a grassy bank make
the tarmac swim, a soft grey pool.
There are limits. Red and white barriers

are down. Maybe it isn't a golf course.
I want the innocuous. Blasts are in my head.
You don't know what size a human
would be in this low country, hardly there.

Too minuscule to hurt.
A given memory, the painting
hangs between experience
and recalling it. It needs us.

Like a violent act. Like a soul
needs a body to learn love,
to bend and touch the ground,
look at the view we've made.

Orpheus Ripple

While I was gone
you ran back into yourself
as water will when a glass has been
taken from and set back down

all bachelor
your body broke
regrouped in rapid time
to the skin of its own meniscus

my hair still wet
the face I had barely shown
pressed against your surface
mirroring itself

till my voice
surpassing muscularity and matter
dipped in through your glass
your silver and you let me sip

Sharing a Park Bench With You
after Frank O'Hara's 'Having a Coke with You'

It is our first Autumn, first holiday and Paris is waiting for our
    timetable of museums and galleries and institutes
and we get up early from the single mattress on the floor of your
    brother's apartment amidst the colony of books
and I don't remember where we have breakfast but your navigation
    is excellent and we could have fitted it all in
but we swing into Agnes B. and you pick me out an expensive coat,
    half-gamine, half-chic and a black turtleneck
and I walk in the mirror for you and buy them both and carry a fat
    white plastic bag into the Jardin de Luxembourg
where we sit in the gentle October sun looking at flowers still blooming
    and the people walking through the green
aisles with a look of important, cultivated leisure and we hold hands
    and kiss and it is hard for both of us to just sit and stare
and not buzz round the sights, suck in paintings and sculptures and
    films like bees visiting these flowers
eking out the last of the season's food, but not to go, to be together,
    warmed in the strolling crowd remains
the image of us I know, return to occasionally because with you,
    the first lover I can share it all with
                                    we do what lovers do
we laze about, looking at Paris relaxing, hovering and at the stunning
    composition of one another's face

Mother in Hospital

Moving towards the old end of the year,
heart burrowed in.
Leaves stencil the pavements,
shadow on a lung.
Breath blown away.
Chest heavy with burrowing heart.
Into dark.
Into amber.
The fall. Falling chest. Rising.
Let it fall. Let it hide.
Rest remain still
in the woolly days.
Looking for a way
to find this season
beautiful. Under the cloud.
A blue morning.
A long low sun
lighting up the neighbour's piano,
its warm wood,
closed lid.
I'd love to see it open.

Chore

After the car accident, dad was given
a brace of pheasants. They hung in the garage,
the females the colour of winter heather,
dull beside the red-eye males,
green throats still gleaming,
iridescent. What swims there?
'They were bred to be shot,' he said.

Days later, the kitchen smelt indecent,
soft bent heads on newspaper.
He wrapped their purple bodies in plastic,
wedged them in the freezer.
As I wiped up the fluff-feathers stuck
to the floor, the edge of the knife drawer,
I wondered if he'd seen the blood I swabbed
from his ears, his bashed scarlet sockets,
his lip like a wattle.

Had he remembered the promise I made
when he said, 'I'm a dead duck'?
'I'll swim with you the next time, anytime you ask
we'll take a dip.' I filled the big hospital bath,
lowered him in, his penis a small water flower,
his word as he lay clean for the first time in days
half floating—Magnificent! he said,
the word immense, healthy as the sea
ripping and repairing on our strand.

Destination: Sleep

Heuston Station
Out of sleep's journey we all travel,
slopey, sleep-dusted on the morning train.
Behind the eyes, black pennies are stacked,
a dull non-seeing, taint of not enough.
Heading west to Europe's edge, my own fleeing,
war at my back, all summer relinquished.
I watch the perishing sky for symptoms,
keeping sleep at vigil's door till the island,
where mountains, unscathed by glaciers
teach you how to thole the howling air.

Newbridge
The train settles, inducing slumber.
A girl's head lolls on an elastic neck,
then rips up with a force seen in torturers.
Public sleeping renders her invisible,
fear of how she looks, surrendered.
The clatter of pennies as daymilk drains
from her eyes. I envy her ease, won't fold,
must eat the newspaper for breakfast.

Tullamore
A brown horse stands by a white-washed wall,
crooked as a bad painting of a horse.

Clara
Men are asleep on the streets of Manhattan
at people's feet, one hand down their jeans,
safely tucked around their sleeping cocks.
No pride, no peril in their slack faces.

The close sky greys like worn bedclothes,

the centre thinning to a smooth pool.
Logo fades on the baggy T-shirt,
the shade of blue ink in an old letter.
The rain comes down, benign as tears,
as universal, blinding, bringing
clarity, softening revenge.
Would all men weep, rinsed in its relief.

Athlone
'Athlone to Galway Line, 150th Anniversary'.
Red and white flags tatter in the wind.
God-Blessed is all a-flutter
in starred and striped reminders
of who invented the freedom to eat.
The guard comes through the carriage counting us,
eleven...twelve...thirteen, on his fingers.
'Dirty weather,' someone says. 'It is that.'
I am comforted by being counted up.
He will notice if I sleep past my stop.

I am counting backwards from one hundred.
At ninety-six, I am counting B1s,
B2s, submarine-launched Tomahawks
and F-15 bombers. Donald Rumsfeld:
the name I'd better get to know. Warplanes
in a Saudi airport stand like racehorses,
white plastic hoods over their cockpits.

Roscommon
Light is stale. The weight and volume of sky.
Silver scrapes the retina. Signs of glare and blare.
A hole as palpable as lust, as hunger.
Fill me up, sleep, stuff me. I'll gorge on dreams,
on dreamlessness. Cardboard cutters.
I'm awake, wide open. Women running like

pale blue birds, unable to fly, clipped,
faces grilled, a book hidden under their arm.
Pennies stand in columns of an ancient city
that will topple if I lay down my head.
Night Kabul, awake for ancestors,
smitten with sleeplessness. Animals find
a warm target when they're tired, circle and
circle and lie down. I uphold an arrow.
The window is cold. Dank. Head won't rest on glass.
It buoys, blurs, prefers to blur. 'It's not long now.
Not worth going to sleep. Sit up, now.'

Castlerea
My body is always cold the first night
in a strange bed. My mother mentioned
recently that the first night she brought me
home, I was fed, put to bed in a cot.
I cried and cried till my grandmother came,
found me foundered, told her that a newborn
cannot generate its own heat. The memory
of coldness still lowers my temperature
when I'm away from home and when
I'm near my mother, I shudder.
'Put her down...' 'She went out like a light.'

Fleeing Europe's west, heading to my own edge.

Head expands and squeezes all at once,
something like the bald, white head of Claude Cahun.
Sleepers ladder into distance; in the window
intervals of fields and bog and treeless hills, broken
stone walls. Spine wants the smooth horizontal
of the train, the sound of reading at bedtime.
Janine Antoni measured the moving eyes of sleep,
sewed its mountain ranges in cloth on a wide loom

to make us a picture of how she dreamt.
It failed. Her sleeping gallery remained locked.
Tilda Swinton slept where all could see her.
But only those who get our blood up
merit being watched: a contented lover,
an ill parent, a child torn by nightmares.

Ballyhaunis
A pillow's weight is the debris of sleep.
Skinflakes collated with dustmite shite.
Poor tossed upon, plumped, flattened pillow,
cornered like a paw under the chin. Flipped.
Punched in rage till you're joyless at daybreak.
No taste for living, for the tiny details
like eyebrows or stamps, or the big ideas
of postmodernity, precision bombing.
No energy to carry or carry on.
Questions of the heart quietly overwhelm.
Temper diminishes, mouth is quarrelsome.
You seek warm dark noiselessness, limblessness,
thoughtlessness, loveless, careless, absconding.
Nothing civic comes from insomnia,
the ache to be off-guard, lulled beyond dying,
forgiven by the recent dead, the coming dead.

Claremorris
A young girl boards the train at Claremorris.
She has Irish eyes, not green and friendly,
rather watery blue with heavy lids,
like she's just been disturbed from racing dreams.
A little sulky, the rims ruddy.
As if she's been crying. Hot, bewildered,
sleepy, startled. Reminds me of a friend
whose nightmare crouched at the foot of her bed
in the dead of night. For once, one hot summer,

41

she woke to find a stranger licking where
her thighs meet. She jolted in alarm, he ran
out the window, rattling the fire escape.
The soft, lowly honouring of a tongue—
an intrusion. It burns a hole like ozone.
A dangerous gaping that makes skin hurt.
It creates a memory you never had
of something that never happened to you.
You want to disbelieve me. It happened.
Her eyes were truth. I checked and felt ashamed
of checking. How long, I wanted to ask,
did he lick before—? I said nothing.
I've dreamt of doing that to a woman.
Waken her by licking. She will pretend
to be sound asleep to keep me at it.
A pact in silence and saliva.
Faked sleep is our cover, our alibi agreed,
a line already drawn in trust.
Hush. My friend gave without knowing
under the diffuse auspices of sleep,
her cunt lapped into confused waking,
by a tampering whose very delicacy
is what shocks and quietly terrifies.

Now, on the fourteenth floor of an apartment block,
even in August, she keeps the windows shut
when she sleeps. But she sleeps.

Manulla Junction
In the *Irish Times* I find a photo
of Osama Bin Laden aged fourteen,
in nineteen-seventy-one in Sweden.
He stands next to a big pink Cadillac,
with twenty-one siblings. The car,
the family, are matched trophies.

Osama is dishy in a skinny-rib jumper,
unabashed in flares, hair long and wavy
as any Osmond, his smile ready
to take on the world. I search
his dark eyes, his stance, for a sign.

Castlebar
Black clouds drag the sky down into the train
hiding from us the tracks of view, of thought.
Breathing slows. Hard rain lashes the window.
There is a sense of warmth.

Edge west to my, fleeing Europe's own heading.

My chest becomes its own curled animal,
breathing its own rhythmic breath.
I won't disturb it. Slowly the whole body
lies down with it, enters its dark vermilion,
our body's common denouement.

I sink to sleep, currency forgotten,
vocabulary absolved, until the journey
is over. An ambrosia of sleep,
creamy, sweet, sustaining, deep,
where doves like snow descend,
covering our gods in this dim high noon,
from the Ardoyne to Jalalabad until
we learn the world, share a stumbling faith
in clear water, sure food, sound sleep.

December 2001

Each Tidy Reverse

Dozy bees bumped at the warm windows.
We tried not to flirt, had said it was over.
You held a hair from your dog to my blind face
like a pin. Each time I detected the prick,
you praised my delicacy, embedded
your green pea beneath my layers of no.

It was adultery that was not. Uncurtained,
invisible, our low drones sealed, you tested
your private syllabus on quiet streets,
slipping loose of the steering wheel, lying
over the handbrake, the gearstick between us
transmitting lust through used air. I grew into
your queen, glass screened with breath, we honeyed
in your car, a hair's breadth from discovery.

Machsom Watch

There is a long line of people standing
in the heat. Air quivers as if through old glass.
Cars are not allowed. Hot dry hills all around.
Orange cabs wait on the other side.

There is a full-length turnstile like the exit
from the Paris Metro, our exit from Nablus
where cars are not allowed. A concrete trench
keeps the line in line, standing in the heat.
One by one we step forward, arms up
like the planes we can't take out of here.
Air quivers like the tip of a rifle.

Our faces must match in the bunker laptop
if we want to shop, go to school,
work, get sick, die over the line,
untraceable in the hot dry hills all around.

The soldier can't read the quietness.
'Hey Elvis, where you off to?' he says.
He wants action and a can of Coke.
The line begins to blur in the heat as if through
old glass, a long people not allowed. 'You
must be Swedish, Osama.' A blond man,
his two kids downy as dandelion clocks, has to smile.
Seeds in his blue eyes drift to the other side,
over the roofs of the cabs, up into the tinder dry hills
    all around.

In My Future

I don't know where I was going when I saw her,
some bus station where I had to change,
where the poor gather, and she's dancing
in a loose sad way like something
caught in a breeze that no one else can feel,
her thin arms rising rising and she spins too slow
to be smooth, too shaky to be graceful
and slowly I realise that she belongs to a group
of young people, black and white, the only mixed group
in the place and they are all unable to keep up
with timetables, currency and destinations,
they hold their stares a little too long,
their heads uncorrected, their faces a touch askew,
but that girl is still dancing for me, for no one,
the most beautiful thing that last year in America
because she was so unaware of herself or anyone else,
so harmlessly expressive, so uncontactable,
so not going to get any more lost.
I carry her pale body, her long fair hair,
a turning ghost of now, the future of my then.

Fair and Lovely
for Michael Langan

Men tuck *paan* parcels into their cheeks,
squirt betel juice on the platform.
The shade narrows and we move closer.
The Madras Mail is late, has been drawing
its diagonal through India for nineteen hours.
A filmstar schoolboy follows my bare shoulders.
I smile instead at the woman in the fuchsia sari
who believes her skin too dark. Her surprise
threads us together. Is the train coming?
The guard's head loops a figure eight.
My presence spruces him up.
I've too much skin, too much light
in my eyes, too many freckles.
The expensive suncream tested by mountaineers
has failed, my chest a lobster. The train is coming.
The crowd rallies. Boys gamble across the tracks.
A woman balancing a bundle teeters down,
sari twisting and hitched. More run from the footbridge
where ads sell the fair-skinned American casuals.
I shove my bag with my foot. Ten, fifteen, twenty
coaches pass. A *chai wallah* bounces off.
A *panni wallah* slithers on. Women chase
the train, cluster at a door, flow on
in a shoal of bright fish, me in their current.

I'm in the Ladies' Compartment.
Women and children bake in soft hot rows,
a hundred eyes on me, the new view,
my jeans, my cropped hair, impossibly male.
The train moves. A space is made. I sit,
flutter my book. No-one else is reading.
A small girl with Cadbury eyes, too shy to look,

clutches a colouring book of fish and elephants.
I dig in my bag, past the loo roll, the mosquito
repellent, the mineral water, Arsen. Alb, plasters,
film, notebook, a bag of Bombay mix, a sanitary pad,
an emergency pound coin, and find it: a green felt-tip.
Her mother shows her how.
She colours up to the very edge. Never over it.
And the whole carriage, now midwives,
praise the green elephant being born.

'Fair and Lovely' is a skin bleach sold in India

Ulster Flutes

Every morning Dad would take us through
a drill. 'Where are we going?' he'd ask.
'Skul,' we'd chime. He'd seize the word,

squeeze it into something a bird sang: 'Schoool!'
and make us repeat it. He worked our 'skul, pull,
butt, flutt' over with a whistle and a rasp, until

the vowels sharpened and quivered
into infinity—'school, pool, boot, flute'.
When these words stuck out—stuck up, alien, ludicrous—

from our sentences, his lips quickly kissed the air:
'Goood.' Years later, over a glass of Cabernet, Dad
talks of the war, when teachers were replaced

by men unfit to fight other men, but strong enough
to make Ulster boys hold their whisht. He recalls
how a master tugged young Dallas from Garvagh

to the front to repeat the word 'flute'. 'Flutt',
said Dallas, as though his ears were waxy,
his tongue starched. He received such a blow

that he fell. 'Flute,' said the master again. Again,
Dallas stood and tried, but 'flutt' was the shape
of a long thin instrument, so 'flutt' emerged

with its own music. The class watched as the master
hit Dallas to the ground for the rest of the lesson
until the boy couldn't leave on his own two feet.

'He never did say "flute",' my father says,
with a sad and tiny awe. All evening, Dallas'
'flutt' plays in my head as it had played in

my father's for over sixty years and I'm sore
for the eleven year old boy he was, whose fear
compressed his lips for the master's words.

Underneath

They walk through the snow forest,
spoiling it as you'd spoil a woman's hair,
wanting to be part of its beauty
and regretting it at the same time.

The sun is hot, sparkling everywhere
and there is a lovely absence of rain,
of noise in general, a rinsed sky,
rinsed ears and eyes, all clearing

before a long narrow riverbed
of snow, which makes them stand
still, go no further and listen
to the sound of running water,

a hidden repair, like love
for the one who is not a lover,
who will go home and not be held.
She can't believe it can be crossed.

Valerie and Her World of Wonders

I pushed a wheelbarrow for you, weighed its lovely balance.
She walks up the paths of her own world.

I hoed weeds, got on my knees, broke roots.
Her pink camellias blow everyone away.

Your mud is under my fingernails.
She speaks Latin because it never hurt her.

I want to watch your top lip move.
Her feet barely touch the ground.

I'd be your breakfast boy, fold down your sheet.
She's all the colours of sand.

You slip through gravel and disappear.
Her blue flowers tilt up to speak.

You plant a passage of gunnera to walk under.
She takes shelter in what belongs to borders.

I want to touch the back of your hand.
She's devoted to the warmth held by soil.

A long line of hearts have tried to blossom for you.
Whoever walks in her garden knows who's master.

I pull away a strand of your hair from my sleeve,
Closer than arm's length, closer than her.

Title from 'Valerie and her Week of Wonders', Czech, Jaromil
Jires, 1970

The Slip Road

When my parents pulled out of the slip road
onto the bypass, it was lashing it down
in dark morning curtains. I heard my mother's
'OK left,' or 'Right, all clear,' or some
direction she's given for over forty years.
Then the gentlest disbelieving wail
and the phone went dead.

I left my body, flew up the length of England
over the Irish Sea to follow all roads
into Belfast, till I was led to them,
their car hit side-on at sixty. Chest
and brain are different injuries, separate
hospitals, no voice or sight of each other
for eleven nights, their longest parting.

My mother hated bothering the staff.
My father asked the Filipino nurse to bring
the nurse. Slowly they came home, drank smoothies
and slept a decade back, each so tender
to the other that we knew they had said
goodbye, then found it wasn't time to leave.
And I, in that dreadful fusing across space,
felt the sharp tug of my beginning, their lives
accidentally pierced and filled with love.

Modern Care of the Erect Self

Up on the wires
above the lake
the mountain takes us in,
cautious not to rock
as if we hold the balance
in our seat, our feet,
bodies mirrored
across our capsule,
among the bells in the forest,
a safe danger,
not knowing what we'll see,
not feeling we must speak,
the swinging space,
pivoted to pinnacle,
lifted through sweetest air
into cloud, the waiting station,
where my skirt is the only one,
where your eyes go soft over fondue
and we walk through droplets,
the ground a fog,
the fall all around,
the last tourists in the world,
the new world comely, close.

Our Geometry, 7th August 2005

You fit
as the perfect square sits
within the perfect circle
a house in the sun I live in
a gift in the moon I open

A clinch
in two diameters
fastens our centre
your four corners a touchstone
for my freehand circumference

The Magic Roundabout

In a room that is now a corridor
in someone else's house, I closed the door
and stamped my feet on the linoleum
that was as turquoise as the gem.
I drummed until noise packed the box:
a present to myself for reaching seven.
In the next room, Dougal in dog-fur coils of icing
waited, and rice-paper yachts on Marie biscuits,
manned by a lone Jelly Baby whose head went first.
I was so puffed up as the day's Queen Bee
I couldn't bear the minute alone it took to pee
and brought the party in there with my racket.

The only other time I spread in headless
sound was that night I cried because I could
not stop, in a tub ringed by yellow plastic.
I cried and rinsed my face, pointless wet
on wet, let out the water, watched it go.
No one came, no one was waiting.
I added hot, a rope that I let burn my feet.
I've never been so finished as in that hideous
honeycomb. Everything in my chest—
lungs, muscles, ribs retching as if to vomit up
the heart, like a baby broken before term.
It was sorrow, yes, but more, it was the disbelief
that the giddy screaming party girl
had sailed three thousand miles to this.

Trá More

                    The beach already had a story
the summer we thought Mum had drowned
with the General in his African teak yacht
and Dad drove frantic around Horn Head
scouring choppy waters. The January light
was failing that last day before London
needed us back and I made you press
into a wind that stretched our cheeks, bloated
our waterproofs across the dunes' steep scallops,
pushing like a continent into the Atlantic's
force, tossing onto the strand in full gale,
the sea all thrash, the sand lumps of shuddering
spume, the view lousy. We turned back,
ready for the Harbour Bar, propelled
top-heavy down the marram paths.

For a final sight of sea, I glanced back
caught dark heads follow fast as if the waves
had hurtled out lost men or dusk delivered
danger of another kind; closer they rose,
surging up the sandhill, a dozen horses,
alight with concentrated life, in charge of wind,
they steadied and stared as we stared
and in a moment's rare equivalency,
neither we nor the horses could tell
if any of us were real.

Warming Up

Snow quietens the hill
at the back like something
that will come to pass
and we know it will.

Words fall all day
making a fuzz in the mind
a line on paper that reads
itself like a new trail.

Then earth comes through
in small wounds, as if pools
of darkness fell from the night
on a white land,

and for a while you cannot
distinguish figure from ground,
features from skin, healing
world from the pain of it.

The First Library

where she learnt   the hush of books
the smell of thinking   as an occupation   she chose
every book by its cover

she sought traces   from other readers   hard
crumbs   a smear of coffee   a stray
hair   marked a page out

in a continuum   stretching right back
to the author herself   a new kind of belonging
given back

spines creased   plastic wiped   a ticket
that entitled her   to a word cord
she could pull on

attached to a bell   that rang   for Carson
in another small town   beckoned
beyond heritage

further than place   and peopled the night
rooms   with something she found
she wanted to do

The Future of Something Delicate

All winter I watched your single cyclamen
unbend its crook
to upflutter in the only light,
letting the light come in
where it could not go itself
to make such pink,
a butterfly asana.
Only now can I begin to feel
how slow your seasons are,
how long buds shepherded
in that crinkled shade,
how much it took to float
your field of veined paths,
to trust some earth.

Holding Pattern

The rope bridge was closed
but we walked with other tourists
to eye its adventure in knots
across the sea to the island.
Volumes of wind
switched back and forth,
moving patches of fast shadow
and gannets steadied their close overlapping
to divebomb the water with a streak
of vertical white, then a burst
of dashed impasto, telling us
how a shoal of fish spread
its lightning body
beneath the swell.
I thought I'd seen it all before
but you, never one to accept
what the surface offers, paused
till the aerial halt and plummet of the seabirds
flared like a long answer in your eyes.
I took your hand as we turned back
so that what passes in the soft collusive
depths between us, what brought
us there, could be made visible
as streams of air, as hunger.

The Trance of Small Gold Flies

The sun has not yet passed behind the wall.
The street is made of mud and shit and piss.
It brings morning to the flowers.
Three children alight on me with a million hands.
The purples, reds, pinks I have planted,
One shows me the wound in his chest.
I have watered, I have fed.
The bandage is dirt-black. He lifts it.
A wasp visits the geranium.
His gash is blue and black and oozing.
I breathe in its slow hovering decisions.
He tugs at it to make it gape like a grimace.
I breathe out the trance of small gold flies.
I try to pull away, hand over my mouth.
The plum tree lets down its branches.
I give him 100 rupees, touch his fingers.
A speckled thrush dips into the birdbath.
My hands burn with fear, swell with bad stories.
I take fifteen minutes of being a garden.
The sky is orange over the Gateway.

Tulip

Splayed spider with sooty feet
caught in a yellow feathered cup,
a wind shuttlecock
blown by softness,
opened by central heating,
expiring in a vase.

Better than to have stayed tight,
bound against the light,
a mouth that never speaks,
no laughter lines,
a forced promise shrinking the heart
slowly from within.

It will exceed itself
as smiling can ache the cheeks,
and lie exhausted, in pieces,
on the table come morning,
strung out, little yellow boats
sailing to Indonesia.

The Far Morning

I don't want to be at the top,
I just want a good view from a flat rock
of the first waves of the day.

They can be mild, pretty curlers,
ripples on a lamb's coat,
waters of a quiet world.

Or crushers, foaming, high-haired,
fit to smother the beach whole,
coming to an easy roll and fade.

Whatever the toss and force,
the rhythm will harness my will,
make my torso one vast lung,

drive the engine of my back
until I move, willing to sprint,
each grain of me grounded.

I don't need wooded inclines
to reach a fierce pinnacle,
give me a long, sandy curve,

air avid with the slippery smell
of oysters, sparked flints, gorse
and the taste of tears,

a place of low hills
and headlands, where a fast walk
into an offshore wind is enough.

Haiku

Bog Gob
  Gutter full of moss
  a tongue where it shouldn't be
  green language of rain.

Non-Attachment
  The cloud is flayed
  by the ridge of Slievemore
  yet it does not rain.

Estuary
  A mackerel sky
  plays in the thinning water
  as sand banks arise.

  A wing of water
  unfolds, fluttering over
  the mirror of trees.

Summer
  I write rapidly
  across the smooth white paper
  amassing freckles.

New Love
  A midge caught in the eyelash
  neither of us sure who
  is the more afraid.

Overcast
No butterflies, bees,
only the dark bulbs of yew
distinct on the lawn.

Dusk
Neighbour's light
star on the mountain
closer than in day.

Solstice
sky, hills, rain, stars
can read what's written
on the ogham stone.

New Year's Eve
under the silence
of the melting snow
standing stone.

Night Sky in Ireland

The first night in the cottage
we discovered utter darkness.
I floated from the bed up and about in it,
my mind unfolding to what it knows.

For you, it took on density and weight,
leant its history on top of you
until your sockets were zeroes.
I thought I could talk you through,
my words a lit path,
show you how to fly blind.
Only your voice rose.

You pleaded to open a slit
in the curtains to let in
the sky from the mountain,
a tree or any kind of shadow.
I did. Your eyes fixed
to that 8 centimetre galaxy
as if the stars could speak.

Next morning, after snow,
the sun played a loud white drum
all over the walls, waking me,
while you slept on and on,
dreaming of Tel Aviv, totting up
your grandfather's numbers.

How to Begin

The teacher was late, the room jam-packed,
everyone sitting on the ground
thinking of what we think we lack.

We rose as he came through the crowd
then re-found our own space.
He scanned our faces, the silence loud.

A young woman stood, left her place,
picked her way through to leave
thinly, at an older woman's pace.

Her face of sorrow made us cleave
and shuffle while we waited,
remembering patience could relieve

the itch, but most of us were sated
with its quiet demand of steady
calm. When she came back a little later

he asked softly was she ready.
'My mind is full of damaged years,'
she said. 'Nothing can quite reach me.'

'Come up here,' he said, 'bring your fears.'
Nothing moved, the room instilled
with the warm burr in the throat of tears.

'Clench your fist,' he said, 'tighter till
your nails make crescents in the skin.'
She squeezed the air with fiercest will.

'Now let go, let go, a deep breath in,'
he showed her an open palm,
showed us how a teaching might begin.

What I'd Love

I

I do it with a dated faith—
search the night sky for a rare conjunction,
wait for a clear moon to distinguish
the knuckle of rings, the red-green glitter,
an intensity closer to the horizon,
reaching from the past into my room's future.

If lovers don't meet in this galaxy, tell me,
is there a last charge before the settling in
to being alone, or just day-to-day, night-by-night
wearing away of the heart until its living doesn't matter?

II

The early evening is full of birds singing.
I am writing. I don't know what else to do with
the blue ruffled lake, wind in the long grass,
low light showing up moss on the sycamore
like warm, new baize. A window of sun falls
across the carpet, hitting my bare toes,
the bed, the brass bed, with blue and white
bedclothes, it seems such a shame to waste.

I'd love sex before dinner, the kind
you don't have time for, immediate and fast,
over before you know it, and you're sitting
at a dinner party, fully dressed, washed
and separate, strings running from you to your lover,
golden, invisible, taut enough to feel every move
but loose enough to allow it,
nostrils packed with the scent bodies make,

seeking ballast in your knife and fork,
wiping the corners of your mouth,
fingers still feral with her juice.

III

Sometimes words carry me, the way cumulus clouds
against the dimmed blue dusk, glide with light,
grand, purposeful, to a place where it's still day.
This evening, they make me wish it was night,
this painful slip out of day, over,
the floating, snowy circumference, pure black.

1994-2005

There's much I felt that I still feel.
Like calling you at three am.
A cut will itch before it heals.

My letters to you will conceal
the impulse from which writing stemmed.
There's much I felt that I still feel.

My phone voice fights to not reveal
the burning source of all my blame.
This cut must itch before I heal.

To apologise you had to kneel.
Camp chivalry could woo this femme.
There's much I felt that I still feel.

Your words were sun that made me peel,
your laugh a weapon that could maim.
A scab grows hard before it heals.

Fear and anger loosed the seal
that fixed our sexy stratagem.
There's much I felt that I won't feel.
Proud flesh is skin that's newly healed.

Among Mountains

You can't believe in dioxins here
  in suicide bombers
     in mindless faith

You can remember to fill your lungs
  trust your neighbour
     know spirit without God

You dance a *pas de deux*
  with a curious deer
     see molehills for what they are

You can meditate on rock
  astride the earth's crust
     make way for lichen

You can feel the prick of childhood
  on nettle walks
     dock leaf coming back to you

You can place the blackened bodies
  on a bank of rose bay willow herb
     let wind take the pink spars' bloom

Other Bodies

There was no cry
even though our thighs were wet
and heat streamed from our starfish.
There were other bodies there,
hurt, bloodied, dying, dead
and in our climbing into each other,
we slipped in amongst them, sticky, inside out.

I didn't want to say I'd gone
under the platform
leaving her in the open
dancing, but her breath followed me,
hands still, lips still,
skin too intact to touch.

She asked where I was,
words ending it, bodies pulled
from the race to renew.
And we lay furled and fastened,
saving it for the streets
in spiked ice cubes.

Then we talked about how to get up,
how to be less Western, how we got
left behind our cunts' innocent drive,
listening to the sirens, for the message,
for the believers who will smoke us out.

Anadyo

I was forty-two before I saw inside
a cancer ward, didn't know no flowers
allowed for fear of bugs and spray.
Carrying them home on the 17,
the Chinese doctor's words dropped on petals
from my silent drum, 'hair loss, nausea,
a ridge in your nails where growth is stalled.'
Hodgkin's Lymphoma cannot be gently put.

They let you burn rosemary, lavender, rose.
You sat cross-legged in a black cord cap,
reading Stanislavsky's 'My Life in Art'.
You've made your home in black, sweetie,
weren't going to give it up for cancer.
I brought you food in handmade bowls,
cutlery and napkins from my kitchen
so you'd mimic me at that white-sheet picnic.

You were clear-throated when the consultant
showed, asked your profession. I resented
his pally-ness, but Greek tragedy lent you dignity
when he said there'd been an error in the reading
of your cells. More rare, less deadly. We crammed
each medical term, trusted statistics. You became
stiller and stiller as if any movement stole energy
from cure and in that calm lay a very young and open

child who never argues—Konstantina,
left too long alone at seven, weighing up
which nasty, boyish act provoked such sickness.
This time you didn't search the source of what,
and I see you now, your body back, your hair
a lustrous black, and the grace that balanced you
when faced with black and white
directs your feet, your hands, your voice.

Café de Noche Vieja

The new mother took the sleeping, bundled baby
from her husband as though it was fallen snow
that would melt in her hands and laid it softly
in its pram where it bawled and both parents drew
close to coo-coo its face but its rasping wails
grew like something locked out that wanted in
and she lifted it, her pale face draining paler
as she patted, walked it, mouth to ear hush-hushing.
At our table, Ersi gestured with her fist
a violent twist, like an ancient woman gives
the scrawny, thrusting neck of some yard bird.
I checked her eyes thinking that I missed
a speck of irony, a flake of fun, but none, our lives'
worst impulse out there with its warm, intoxicating lure.

Behindhand
on the 60th anniversary

The dog's bark is all the fear we don't shout
at the dark, stones thrown to the waning moon.
Each morning, you take the train under,
without heart, plugged into other people's music,
lunch wrapped in your bag, too good-girl to need
the word for arrears we learnt from the crossword.

Yesterday, before we got up, fingers tapping the beat
on my bum, you sang a new melody, the Shabbat song
for a used-up dream, tuning hate's echo to a round
dark cadenza. 'This is your true work,' I should've said,
but sorrow caught in my throat, like something too big
to swallow, swallowed down those tracks lit by a mile of fire.

All night in that top floor flat in Amsterdam, I'd listened
for a stifled cough, a page turned in the attic, held you closer,
kept seeing you unsteady on a big black bicycle, your face
monochrome, until you pedalled, not knowing
how to turn or stop, your smile breaking
and breaking the street into colour.

The Good Marriage

I wore a bikini while I worked
and pink flip-flops, took a shovel and folded back
the mass of rotten food, remains
of last winter's parings. Lip-coloured worms shrank
from sunlight in a viscous living tangle.
Avocado stones rolled up, resilient to dark.

I dug in, lifted the damp meal
into a tin bowl, took it to the centre of the garden,
sat with it, began to sift. It had its own heat,
clean as low-tide sand. I thought of the bargain
made as each grain, processed by a tube of worm had
glistened out with a newness that could feed.

I rubbed light into it, thought
I wouldn't mind becoming this, under someone's nails.
I packed a window box, poked in rocket seeds,
enclosed them. I watered, waited, watered.
I watched green show, sprout hundreds of tiny beads,
then run over itself in long, thin tails.

It never fattened, frilled or served
our summer plate. The compost was too rich,
                    my neighbour said.
I'd never heard of such a thing as too much goodness.
Now, thinking of you and me, our sweet flower bed,
to survive, must we introduce some rocks,
bury broken crockery between us and a bit of dirt?

Cashelkeelty

A close green wood
shiny with rhododendron,
a path over scuffed roots,
a smell of rain.

A river white with tumble,
boulder-edged. A stile.
A valley suddenly, a bowl
of mountains, the sky.

A new wooden bridge. Thank you.
A track of beaten grass.
A climb to the rim,
a great lung balanced at its head.

Steady, each gene reaches
to touch its start, this first art,
the first, outlasting praise
of taking breath.

The Funnel

The time of the sparrows, their ratchet of sound
an unoiled mechanical panic. 'Hurry home,'
they say. 'Kiss quick. Drink. Dance. What
a calamity. It's too late.' All the day's undoing
in their beaks closing in as the land throws peaches
into the sky and a Turner unfolds overhead
in gold and baby blue and a pink she couldn't wear.
Clouds build a Sahara—sand rivers and ridges
no foot will ever touch. Are we compelled to watch
eye to eye with one great art to practise dying?

Litter scatters over the mountain, an open torso
dried out and bloodless. Three lights spring up
on a bungalow. Tail lights pick out the road
I followed, a red ball rolling down a gutter.
Her face after the dance performance,
bodies in tableaux of every human pain,
grotesque and gullible on that ledge of love.
She looked blasted as this landscape and pretty
and I was glad to have her, uncopied, not as a picture
or as the image I have of her face at the edge
of the earth, after too much consciousness, her eyes
shut, lips baring the night song she's worked
from the days without colour, coming back alive
for those who have found sense in grey.